C000145781

Terrace

Terrace
Richard Skinner

Smokestack Books
1 Lake Terrace, Grewelthorpe, Ripon HG4 3BU
e-mail: info@smokestack-books.co.uk
www.smokestack-books.co.uk

Text copyright 2015, Richard Skinner, all rights reserved.

ISBN 978-0-9929581-5-2

Smokestack Books is represented
by Inpress Ltd

Acknowledgements

Thanks are due to the editors of the following print and online publications in which some of these poems first appeared: *Amaryllis, And Other Poems, Brand, HARK, The Interpreter's House, Magma, Pieced Work* and *Writers' Hub*. Thanks also to Wayne Burrows for his editorial suggestions, to Martin O'Neill for the artwork and to Andy Croft at Smokestack. 'My grandmother's things' was selected for publication in the *Rhyme & Reason* 2015 diary. Both 'Il ritrovamento di Giuseppe' and 'Two Views of the Lacemaker' were shortlisted for the Charles Causley Competition. 'Parma Violets' was shortlisted for the Wenlock Poetry Festival Competition and longlisted for the National Poetry Competition. 'Epithalamium' contains elements of 'Marina' & 'Usk' by TS Eliot.

'*What I need today is not a book and movement forwards:
I need a destiny, and grief as heavy as red corals.*'
Viktor Shklovsky

Contents

The Structure of Magic

for Christian

Clear your throat and assume the pose.
Reject the Romantic in your heart.
Use tacks and hangers to pin up your dreams,
but remember, the map is not the territory.
Learn to stand alone, like a magus on an island.
It is not enough to manage love; you must express it, too.
It is better to be too sweet than too sour.
Never be the man who fails to recognise himself,
but if you steal, steal well. Cover your tracks.
The place of salvation is small, maybe just a window,
and bear in mind that time is only time's lapse.
Always leave yourself an exit plan
for choice is the only freedom.
Be senescent. Don't admire. Refuse.

Parma Violets

Among the colonnades, Count Pierre stalks and surveys
the blooms. He must select the best-sized to abscond to Genoa,
where a boat awaits for England. The tiny petals bugle
their lilac time. Blurry, tribal. They say they are sterile.

He has heard it said that love can grow
inside one, no matter how rough the ground,
just as a twig thrown into a salt mine will, after many years,
come out crystalline.

Karen Philpott and I would meet behind her estate
on the wasteland. Her bloodless face, her hair straggly, unkempt.
She gave me a Parma Violet and I placed it on my tongue. It
    tasted of iron.
She said it was OK because she used them like the pill.

They say the yews here can 'walk' by dropping branches,
which then take root and become a trunk.
Diving into the ground head-first, the cemetery is never still.
They say a yew can walk an acre a year.

Scent of Magnolia

In this bored park, green has turned yellow, all night
nacreous petals of magnolia have dropped.
Tired old sparks that refuse to ignite;
the faulty machines have finally stopped.

You are further away, on an aphasic shore,
a figure locked in the pattern of a wall.
The metallic surface, sulphur-like in the sun,
renders the paper ineffectual.

Children play, dogs chase, the ball is always thrown
out of reach. On and on they run,
stirring the petals from the sleepy floor,
reciting old speeches in abandoned halls.

Indoor Pallor

You sip your mint tea while I study your profile:
the imperious nose, the predatory eye.
We sit a long way from the ruby walls,
the ceiling rose off centre, the white plasterwork far too high.

You discard your tea. I used to wonder why
the sea was blue at a distance, yet green close up,
and colourless in my hands.
A lot in life is learning to like blue.

In the driveway, the people carrier crunches on gravel.
You are the blue light in a block of ice,
hinted at, but never seen, the only force
shivering with enough energy to escape.

We both know, this time, there is no turning back.
You clutch your throat in the wicker chair,
for a moment recognising me.
You wait for the men to come, with rouged lips,
brace yourself for the arms and the turn of a lock.

The Owl

Athena eyes, ice-scoop head.
Three talons that grip
tight as a baby's fingers.

How I fear you – your wisdom,
your patience, the silent swoop, the
kazoo scream in the night.

Budgerigar

Your breast is a map
of Madagascar,
a stain of salmon red
on chartreuse green.

Your head is a helmet,
a medallion fit
to pierce any iron-
clad armour.

You swarm from the west,
a badge that augurs
pestilence, chatter, the long day
closed tight in the heart.

Plaza San Miguel Bajo, Granada

for J

And so, after walking back and forth along the cobbles,
we found the lost square,
its tables prowled by slit-eyed cats.
We sat under a street lamp.
As dusk grew, the *golondrinas* flew tightly around trees,
stitched together huge tracts of air
into books entitled *You Are Not Here*.

How clear the night was.
The orange lamp outlined your head
as an afro halo, which I later embraced.
In bed, I hoped my sleep would be dreamless.
I longed to surrender
to the faultless workings of days,
the sense of falling.

Down in the *huertas*, the wind builds,
moves into the city, ruffles the backs of poppies,
branches of honeysuckle,
buffets the Alhambra's tall walls.
The palace feels nothing, at ease with the ether,
its flags blowing as if to say, *'I am here,
I am here, and am not going away.'*

Isola di San Michele, Venice

'to step on an island is to die...'

It took me an age to find you,
your final port of call
obscured by a turmoil of long grass and eucalyptus.
On the mossy slab, the words:
EZRA POVND.
Each glyph sharp as a knife,
cut to the bone.

The sun beats, peacocks cry,
pansies shrivel in the heat.
Each of these *cimitero* is like a Chinese character
legible only from the sky.
Who reads them now?
Just the birds, who, passing over, break flight
and drop like a stone to the ground.

'*Il ritrovamento di Giuseppe*'

a painting by Lazzarro Bastiani (1449-1512)

Voices raised in unison,
hands held in prayer,

they kneel and feign fealty
to the ghost, eyes blank as coins.

Their black pantaloons are amazed, ochre
on ochre. In the fading light,

they see no beauty, only opportunity.
Behind stand oleanders. Further still,

on a faint horizon, the miry earth, half-
eaten skulls lay whitened in marigold-fields.

Manganese in Deep Violet

Down on the waterfront I watch
Africans in green overalls

sweep and clean the quays,
further out on the Thames

boats bring syphilis and smallpox
upriver from Dutch colonies.

Much further downstream I step
into Tate Modern,

look at the Heron and feel the unease
overlapping water colour, in the Hall

the footfall of probable futures
quickens, and fear comes rushing in.

The Monarch Foundation

On their arrival, we tell our guests that what cannot be remembered cannot be left behind. The maps of fields they have crossed to get here are engraved on their souls. This is our fight, our contest. We say to them, 'Something abolished internally will return from the outside in the form of a delusion'.

In their off-white rooms, they stare at the floating speech bubbles and nod in agreement. Our mission statement seems to work. They repeat, 'One can only know what one already understands.' If they do not understand, we refer them to the Charteroak Foundation, in Schenectady, New York.

All of our guests suffer quietly, mostly at night. We tell them not to worry, that a phobia is a form of protection. In one rare case, our narcissistic guest had a fear of white shirts, which made things difficult, momentarily. We continued to cross check at night and hid the knives. We recovered.

In our experience, neurotics build castles in the air, but psychotics live in them. This is the greatest lesson of all. We are busy constructing those towers and crenelations on a bed of white light under leaves. Our results will be published soon and, until then, we will take no further questions. Thank you.

Orpheus

When I emerged from the shadows,
I should have seen light,
but saw instead a deeper black.
Since then, it has been a struggle,
the mornings weightless, cramped,
my life stuffed into a sour gift.
I can no longer sit still. That failure dreams me.
The girl, pale and thin,
her vacant stare at my expectant back.
I remember walking towards the trees, and beyond,
the red chapel, where we were to marry.
In that last turn, I carried with me the earth's spin.
I should have foreseen my failure,
should have been dutiful, as they say I am,
but there was a sense of falling,
and I knew the song in the seashell
had melted away like foam.
Everything is clear now. Then, the land above
was nothing but pure illusion,
and I understood this as I rose to the surface,
gulping air but losing love.

Nefertiti

for J

From the opened gates of Ophir,
owls, cuckoos, asses and dogs tumble.
Apes clamber over sands,
peacocks screech and fly into acacias.

Later, Nebuchadnezzar exited with all the gold,
sandalwood and ivory in the world,
razed Jerusalem, went mad
and ate grass.

Then Samson left, his hair shorn,
and ended up eyeless in Gaza.
'Once I moved about like the wind.
Now I surrender to you and that is all.'

Watching all this is Nefertiti,
her bronze brow at odds with the sun.
She basks in the warmth to stir
the *sangue dormido* in her veins.

In her eyes, flecks of mica sparkle.
They have the look of possession,
like in the eyes of women
for their men and children.

She smells of neroli, of orris butter,
the roots of Iris – floral,
obscenely fleshy, like the odour
beneath a breast or between buttocks.

She attracts civet cats, which sit at her feet.
She pays no mind. She is a sphinx without a secret,
a colossal ennui who, like an elephant,
has an appointment with the end of the world.

Pillar

High Level Route

I

Leaving the alluvial fan-
head of Wasdale, we cross the bridge
and enter the arena
of undulating dale and, higher,
a radial of ridges from Pillar.

II

At fifteen-hundred feet, the air
has been sucked out the dale,
tussocks of teasel quiver in the breeze. Clouds,
like bits of fleece, lour.

III

Up on Looking Stead,
the bog water tremors, the curd-like scum
laps against stone, clags on grass.
A sheep's skull – sun-worn, wind-greyed – lies half in, half
out the tarn,
its loose teeth chocking in the jaw.

IV

The light on the east face
is dismal – far below,
a valley of dark conifers creeps up the elbow
of Ennerdale,
like a mange.

V

We leave the gorse and grass and
enter the domain of rocks.
Like a whetstone when dry – in rain,
they are slick as a typesetter's box.

VI

After Pisgah, we are just shy of the top.
Clouds disperse and light blooms in arcs,
the rocks become luminous,
the sky like bits of blue material,
yet still immaterial. And the sun shines
like a yolk broke on tin,
filling us with yellow after all that black.

Cumbria Lumen

Light seeps fast over the dun fells
like a great curtain of yellow
opening to reveal the sky, the fields.
A vast migraine, coming forwards, stuns
and sweeps through us like a broad sword,
leaves us as topheavy aerials,
quivering, looking for the *arc au ciel*
far behind in summer rain.

Death in a French Garden

Pear tree, quince tree,
bottle of curaçao.
Chicken fricasses, veal, mutton, chitterlings with sorrel.

A rosary. Hands like leather.
Fichu, fire-dogs,
nonpareil arabesques.

Espaliered apricots, hawthorn hedge, speedwells,
slate sundial on a brick pedestal,
eglantines, spruce bushes,
sprays of honeysuckle and clematis.

Clumps of nettles surrounding the great stones,
blotches of lichen.

Soup à la bisque, au lait d'amandes.
Coping of a wall.

White roses,
blush roses,
white musk roses,
damask rose.

Valerian and camphor baths,
Vichy, Seltzer, Barège waters,
Raspail patent medicine,
Regnault paste,
Darcet lozenges.

The Jars

I   Stigmat.Croci

Brittle larrikins, burnished tongues.
Crimson stigmas whose carpals
tickle the back of the throat.

Their idioform-smell of hospitals;
the crocin both a taste and a stain.

Throw back your head to furnish
the flow of amber sticks,
the flood of twig-blood.

II   Cort.Rad.Ipecac.Pulv.

Mashed roots for stomach complaints,
rhizzomes that singe and sting.

An emetic tannin for the night sweats,
bulemic feints, opiate daze.

Lean over and brace the gut
for the nuclear rumble and spew
of syrupy mush and pulp.

Two Views of the Lacemaker

'He passed her by, very close, without seeing her. Because she was one of those souls who makes no sound but who must be patiently sought, whom one must know how to see. In bygone days, an artist would have seen her as a seamstress, water-carrier or a lace-maker.'

I

A water-carrier in whom she patiently sought
bygone days without souls.

Seeing her, he makes no sound.
An artist would know of her,
have passed her by,
see as be seen.

How very close, one who was
a lace-maker,
or seamstress.

To those who must
because one must.

II

Days must have passed, must be sought.
Was no one seen very patiently?
How? In whom?

Because without seeing her
he would know her;
as to her –
she makes those see by sound.

A water-carrier, one lace-maker, a seamstress –
bygone souls of an artist.

Three Landscapes

I

Sunrise blow-
torch throbs
in eyes.

Birth becomes wrath.
Things burn,
filth expires.

This death by
scorching
punishes us
but
purifies.

II

Golondrinas dart,
unpick
ideas for
Kasper
and Idriss
in an
incandescent dusk.

III

Malaga at night:
a cluster of wet diamonds
tossed on blue velvet.

Sonar

A man sweeps a field
armed with a metal detector,
the plate aching to find
the sternum bone or shield
of some Saxon lord and protector.

My radar reaches three feet
and searches for the band
dropped somewhere long ago
after losing all the heat
and the half-life of your hand.

The eyes of a submariner
lock on the ghostly green ring
as the sonar scans the immensity,
his finger presses on the monitor
and ricochets into the ocean, one long single ping.

My grandmother's things

i.m. Vera Ethel Skinner, née Pitcher, 1912-2009

A brown bakelite telephone
with separate handpiece, Leicester 58803.
Her mother's newspaper
cuttings, a wooden letter rack.
Wooden mushroom, needles – darners & sharps.
Royal Worcester milk jug
shaped out of fronds, a bone-
handled knife.
A wind-up cheese grater, a colander, egg
poacher and steamer pan.

Epithalamium

for Christian & Liz

Water flows downhill. We must always swim to the source,
 sometimes against the tide.
We are born tilted, and by its weight, our body moves towards its
 proper place.
Migration is a way of coping with the tilt. We have seasons.
Ferrous browns, ash greys, sunlit oranges. My love is my weight.

The swifts flit at dusk. They swoop, roll, dip like blades.
They slice the air, scour out the inside of a sphere.
You get strong shadows with a strong life. The lighter the surface,
the darker the depths. The shallow murmur but the deep are
 dumb.

There is a red streak in the west, but mostly the sky is a cold,
 liquid blue.
Time courses through us like water. Two bodies rise in the night
 sky, Venus and Sirius, the dog star.
Together they are very bright and very near.

You are more distant than stars and nearer than my eye. Lift your
 eyes gently,
but not too deep, to a place where all the waters meet,
where the birds gather in the shadows, and I will find you there.